Farm Anima[ls]

Chickens

by Betsy Rathburn

BLASTOFF! Beginners

BELLWETHER MEDIA
MINNEAPOLIS, MN

Blastoff! Beginners are developed by literacy experts and educators to meet the needs of early readers. These engaging informational texts support young children as they begin reading about their world. Through simple language and high frequency words paired with crisp, colorful photos, Blastoff! Beginners launch young readers into the universe of independent reading.

Blastoff! Universe ★

Reading Level

Grade K

Grades 1-3

Grade 4

Sight Words in This Book 🔍

a	get	many	too
and	go	on	up
are	good	the	
be	have	their	
can	in	these	
eat	is	they	

This edition first published in 2024 by Bellwether Media, Inc.

No part of this publication may be reproduced in whole or in part without written permission of the publisher. For information regarding permission, write to Bellwether Media, Inc., Attention: Permissions Department, 6012 Blue Circle Drive, Minnetonka, MN 55343.

Library of Congress Cataloging-in-Publication Data

Names: Rathburn, Betsy, author.
Title: Chickens / by Betsy Rathburn.
Description: Minneapolis, MN : Bellwether Media, 2024. | Series: Blastoff! Beginners: Farm Animals | Includes bibliographical references and index. | Audience: Ages 4-7 | Audience: Grades K-1
Identifiers: LCCN 2023039740 (print) | LCCN 2023039741 (ebook) | ISBN 9798886877588 (library binding) | ISBN 9798886879469 (paperback) | ISBN 9798886878523 (ebook)
Subjects: LCSH: Chickens--Juvenile literature.
Classification: LCC SF487.5 .R38 2024 (print) | LCC SF487.5 (ebook) | DDC 636.5--dc23/eng/20230831
LC record available at https://lccn.loc.gov/2023039740
LC ebook record available at https://lccn.loc.gov/2023039741

Editor: Elizabeth Neuenfeldt   Designer: Laura Sowers

Printed in the United States of America, North Mankato, MN.

Table of Contents

A New Day

Cock-a-doodle-do!
The rooster
is calling.
Wake up!

What Are Chickens?

Chickens are birds.
Males are roosters.
Females are hens.

rooster

hen

Chickens have **feathers**. They can be many colors.

feathers

Chickens have **combs**. They have **wattles**.

comb

wattle

They have
pointy mouths.
They peck
their food!

Life on the Farm

Chickens live
on farms.
They go outside.

They eat seeds.
They eat plants
and bugs, too!

seeds

plants

bugs

Hens lay eggs.
Farmers get
the eggs.

eggs

farmer

These chickens are tired. They sleep in a **coop**. Good night!

coop

Chicken Facts

Parts of a Chicken

comb

pointy mouth

wattle

feathers

Life on the Farm

eat

lay eggs

sleep in coops

Glossary

combs

flaps of skin that stick up on the heads of chickens

coop

a farm building for chickens

feathers

soft coverings on chickens

wattles

red skin on the necks of chickens

23

To Learn More

ON THE WEB

FACTSURFER

Factsurfer.com gives you a safe, fun way to find more information.

1. Go to www.factsurfer.com.

2. Enter "chickens" into the search box and click 🔍.

3. Select your book cover to see a list of related content.

Index

The images in this book are reproduced through the courtesy of: Tsekhmister, cover, p. 7; Aksenova Natalya, p. 3; Robert Adamec, pp. 4-5; johannviloria, p. 6; tea maeklong, p. 8; andrea lehmkuhl, pp. 8-9; Potapov Alexander, p. 10; Dora Zett, pp. 10-11; driftlessstudio, pp. 12-13; deepblue4you, pp. 14-15; GOLFX, p. 16; jelenaaaaa.p, pp. 16-17; avoferten, p. 17; Ernie Cooper, p. 17; lovelyday12, p. 18; Mint Images Limited/ Alamy, pp. 18-19; Peter Klampfer, p. 20; :csmorrell, pp. 20-21; Thyrymn2, p. 22; Dudarev Mikhail, p. 22 (eat); kevin leah, p. 22 (lay eggs); CHARTGRAPHIC, p. 22 (sleep in coops); Mircea Costina, p. 23 (combs); ENRIQUE ALAEZ PEREZ, p. 23 (coop); Imageman, p. 23 (feathers); vPaulTech LLC, p. 23 (wattles).